HOMESCHOOLING, AUTISM STYLE

RESET FOR SUCCESS

WENDELA WHITCOMB MARSH, MA, BCBA, RSD

with SIOBHAN MARSH

HOMESCHOOLING, AUTISM STYLE

All marketing and publishing rights guaranteed to and reserved by:

FUTURE HORIZONS INC.

(800) 489-0727
(817) 277-0727
(817) 277-2270 (fax)
E-mail: info@fhautism.com
www.fhautism.com

ISBN: 9781885477835

This book is dedicated to
all the families who are homeschooling, autism-style.
Hang in there! You can do this!

It's also for our family, Anne and Noel,
and in loving memory of
David Scott Marsh.

CONTENTS

ACKNOWLEDGMENTS...VII

INTRODUCTION IX

PART I: START 1
Chapter 1: READY Plan for Success (Get it Down on Paper) 3
Chapter 2: SET Prepare for Success (Gather Your Materials) 9
Chapter 3: GO Path to Success (You're Good to Go!) 15

PART II: HAMMOCK 21
Chapter 4: HEART Activities That Speak to Kids' Feelings 23
Chapter 5: ACTION Activities That Get Kids Moving..........................33
Chapter 6: MIND Activities That Get Kids Thinking 35
Chapter 7: MUSIC Activities That Sing 41
Chapter 8: OUTDOORS Activities That Get Kids Out of the House..45
Chapter 9: CHORES Activities That Get the Job Done 49
Chapter 10: KITCHEN Activities That Put Food on the Table 53

PART III: ACT...57
Chapter 11: VARIED Vote, Alternate, Recharge, Improvise, Empower, Dare...59
Chapter 12: FUN ACTIVITIES Frequent, Unscheduled, New............63

PART IV: KIDS 67
Chapter 13: DISTRACTIBLE DORY......................................69
Chapter 14: HYPER-FOCUSED HERMIONE.....................................73
Chapter 15: CREATIVE CALVIN 77

PART V: END 81
Chapter 16: The End of the Book..83

HELPFUL BOOKS..89

ACKNOWLEDGMENTS

This book came together so quickly, our heads are still spinning. Wendela is grateful to Siobhan for the idea to write this book, for the strong push to do it, and then for agreeing to co-author it. It's so much better because of you! Thanks to our sister/aunt Cynthia Whitcomb, who proofread every chapter as quickly as we could write them. Thanks to Anne and Noel, who were supportive and encouraging while we focused on this book to the exclusion of just about everything else.

We are especially grateful to Future Horizons president Jennifer Gilpin Yacio and managing editor Rose Heredia-Bechtel. When we emailed Rose with this idea, we got a Yes on the same day. Now, barely two weeks later, we have a finished book, rushed to print for all the families who need this information now rather than six months from now. Thank you to everyone on the Future Horizons team, who went above and beyond during difficult times to help provide guidance to these families. You are awesome!

INTRODUCTION

"I will get my education—if it is in home, school, or anyplace."

— Malala Yousafzai

If you're a parent of a school-aged child with autism spectrum disorder (ASD), you already know something about homeschooling. You may have been homeschooling all along, or it may have come as a surprise when your child's school was closed due to COVID-19 health and safety concerns. Perhaps your family is still sheltering at home. You've learned to manage physical distancing, face masks, and frequent handwashing; however, your child's school may not be ready to reopen for face-to-face learning yet. If they are open but you have family members at risk, you may have chosen a home-learning option. Even if your child is able to attend school regularly during the week, they might benefit from some school-like structure during weekends and holidays. You may even be embarking on a hybrid learning journey. Whatever your reasons, you're looking for homeschooling support, autism-style.

First, go easy on yourself. Don't worry about your child falling behind academically. Everybody is facing the same situation, and no one should point a finger or blame parents if your child didn't do every worksheet provided by their teacher. Your child's safety and happiness are your primary responsibility and should be your focus right now. Love them unconditionally, hug them when they need a hug, and keep them happily occupied. Children learn all the time, not just when they're sitting at a desk with a book in front of them.

One thing children learn is discerning when they're being lied to. It's not necessary to share every statistic that keeps you up at night, but don't say "Everything's fine" when they can tell you're worried. Knowing that their grownups are worrying about something they won't talk about makes it seem like it must be too terrible for words. Their anxiety may spike as a result, and they may act out their confusion behaviorally. Some may start doing things you haven't seen in a long time, like bed-wetting, babyish behavior, and two-year-old "tantrums" which are really autistic meltdowns. This is perfectly normal and to be expected. Kids who don't have autism are also doing some of these things all around the world right now. Whatever your family situation and whatever your child's needs, it's time to step up your parent-as-teacher game now.

The book you're holding was written by an autism educator, Wendela, and her daughter Siobhan, who homeschooled herself while growing up in an autism-majority family. Siobhan's Strategies throughout the book show her unique perspective and the tips and tricks that worked for her. You'll find in this book the structure and strategies you need to help you get through this time of homeschooling, autism-style.

So, let's start.

PART I

START:

Schedule Theme-based Activities at Routine Times

"Whatever you can do, or dream you can, begin it.
Boldness has genius, power, and magic in it."
— *Johann Wolfgang von Goethe*

CHAPTER 1: READY

Plan for Success (Get it Down on Paper)

> "All things are ready, if our mind be so."
> — William Shakespeare

Your child's sense of security may be affected by a need for structure. This is something you can give them, but you need to get ready before you can start. And when I say start, I mean *START: Schedule Theme-based Activities at Routine Times*. Get your themes and ideas ready and in writing before you start teaching. Don't try to wing it; it never goes well. You'll thank yourself later if you plan in advance exactly which theme-based activities you will schedule routinely throughout your child's day. Write it down!

CALENDAR IT

Get yourself a lesson-plan book or calendar with plenty of room to write. Plan the subjects you'll need to include as part of the grade-level requirements. One important thing to realize is that a homeschool day is not nearly as long as a traditional school day. Do not, no matter your child's grade level, schedule them to do coursework from 8:00 AM to 3:00 PM five days a week. Remember, in a traditional classroom, the teacher has 30 kids to manage, teach, and try to keep on task. If your child is older, you might ask them how much time they think they spent per subject sitting around bored, waiting for their classmates to catch up, or doing what they consider pointless busywork. Now is your chance to redesign the school day to meet your child's specific needs.

SIOBHAN'S STRATEGIES: Individualize their schedules. Is one child a night owl who doesn't really hit their stride until noon? Schedule a lighter morning of stretching and creative activities, and save the academics for after lunch. Do you have a lark who is up and ready to go at the break of dawn but becomes sluggish in the afternoon? Get all their heavier subjects out of the way first thing, and schedule the fun stuff later. You can probably finish a day's worth of academics in 2-3 hours for grade school kids and 3-4 for middle and high school. For the rest of the day, they can work on things that inspire them, free reading, outdoor time, and physical activity. You may even restructure their day to allow sleeping in or taking a nap. Sleep is critical for children's brains and health, and we're all struggling to get good sleep these days.

Write down what they will learn or do at each time slot, divided hour by hour (or half-hour by half-hour for younger children or those with shorter attention spans). Alternate different kinds of activities when possible so they don't feel stuck in a rut. Writing it down will give you guidance as you go through your days. Don't carve the calendar in stone, though. Be prepared to modify the schedule as you go along and learn what works best for your child. If your child needs to take a "mental health day" and finish their work over the weekend, there's no reason they can't.

THEME-BASED ACTIVITIES

Why should your activities be theme-based? Themes help children cognitively link learning activities together. Kids often enjoy making connections and expanding their learning across subjects. Plus, it's fun to have special theme-based days to anticipate when you can't get out like you used to. Maybe Pajama Day doesn't sound like much fun when you're home all day, but consider the following:

> *Sundae Sunday.* Get creative with ice cream toppings for dessert or make a "surprise sundae" for dinner using savory foods that look like components of an ice cream sundae, such as mashed potatoes or cottage cheese as ice cream, gravy as chocolate fudge, and marinara as strawberry syrup. Can they fool you into thinking it's a dessert? They'll have fun trying! To target academics, ask them to write out recipes or let them create math word problems related to sundaes, such as "If I make a sundae with 25 scoops of ice cream and there are 5 people in the family, how many scoops will each person get?"

> *Museum Monday.* Find a virtual museum field trip online to explore as a family. Alternatively, let each child check out a separate museum independently and report to the family at dinner what they saw. Consider having them make impromptu commercials to convince others to check out the museum they toured. Let the kids make a museum of their own. Maybe they'll find artifacts of past family vacations to display in the form of photos and souvenirs. Let them get artistic and create masterpieces, drawing or constructing cardboard frames for their paintings. A natural history museum at home might have stuffed animals posed against drawings of their natural environments. If your child is studying a particular period in history for social studies, making a historical museum about it will support their academics. Whatever topics are covered in science for their grade level can find their way into a Museum of Science and Technology right in your living room. Based on their skills, children can either write or dictate descriptive signs for each display, and your tech-savvy kids might record an audio-tour the family can listen to as they view the museum.

> *Good Newsday Tuesday.* Read and report on or write only good news. Avoiding potentially distressing news while the kids are up will help

your family's stress levels, and good news stories are always appreciated. Your older children who can safely and responsibly navigate the internet may be asked to find good news or cute animal videos to share with the family. They can try writing an article from the family pet's point of view about what they saw on a walk or out the window. You might all get together and write your own family newspaper to share with relatives and friends. You will find many free options for creating online newsletters. Imagine how thrilled the grandparents will be to get each edition!

➤ *Friendsday Wednesday.* This is a good day to keep in touch with friends, classmates, cousins or pen pals. When it's safe to do so, plan physically distanced outdoor play dates. Alternatively, consider setting up Zoom-type meetings with friends, drawing and sending pictures, or sending emails. You can schedule a video call with your child's BFF or grandparent. Try creating a code using emojis, such as an apple icon to represent the letter A, so they can send secret messages to their pen pal.

➤ *Fursday Thursday.* If you have pets, this is the day to pamper them. Go on extra walks with the dog, toss the ball, or play tug-of-war with a rope toy. Let the kids make a fishing toy for the cat by attaching a string or length of elastic to the end of a short dowel, chopstick, or any stick. Then attach a small cat toy or yarn pompom to the end of the string. Watch your cat leap and stretch as your child makes the toy dance and swing around. If you don't have pets and your kids love animals, ask a local no-kill animal shelter if they need volunteers to socialize kittens or play with puppies. Many shelters encourage children to read aloud to the animals, which can improve your child's reading confidence while reducing stress. Are stuffed animals more your kid's speed? They can read aloud to their toys, especially if they have a book that teaches them facts about that animal. You can also take a virtual trip to a zoo or aquarium. Some have regular television shows or videos, and many have a webcam live feed so you can see what the penguins or otters are up to.

> **Fan Fiction Friday.** Have your kids write a story or draw a comic about their favorite fictional character. They may be happier writing a paragraph about a video game character or superhero than doing a generic writing task from a textbook. If the result is the same, with an opening sentence, supporting sentences, and a conclusion, then why not let them write fan fiction? They are honing their writing skills while they pursue their passion. You can help them make a cover for their work and put it on their shelf alongside the real deal.

> **Flatterday Saturday.** This is a good day to flatter your family members by giving appropriate compliments. Everyone loves to be noticed and appreciated, and it's a good social skill to develop. You can model gracefully giving and receiving compliments. The home is a safe space to learn and practice which compliments are appropriate and which may make people feel uncomfortable. Try focusing on compliments about something a person did rather than their physical appearance.

ROUTINE TIMES

Why should you schedule activities at routine times rather than just letting your child do whatever they want, whenever they want to? One reason is that a schedule is something your child is probably used to at school. Familiarity can be comforting. Another reason is that many children engage in fewer problem behaviors when they have a schedule to return to. Finally, a schedule is an anchor to keep them hooked into their day rather than floating aimlessly. If your child is perfectly happy to glide through their day with no set activities, if they create learning experiences for themselves, and if they don't have melt-downs that could be caused by lack of structure, then you may not need to schedule activities for them. However, many, if not most, children with ASD appreciate the comfort of knowing what they can expect throughout their day, and they do better when they have a schedule.

For most children, you can model their daily schedule after the schedule they had in school. This helps the transition from school-based to home-based education, and if they return to the classroom later, it will make that transition easier, too. There are always exceptions to this rule, but it's better to start out with a schedule and then add more flexibility, than to start out with no schedule and regret it later.

You're off to a good start, scheduling theme-based activities at routine times. Now, get that beautiful plan down on paper. You're ready to homeschool, autism-style!

CHAPTER 2: SET

Prepare for Success (Gather Your Materials)

"He who is best prepared can best serve his moment of inspiration."

— Samuel Taylor Coleridge

Before you're ready to go on your homeschooling adventure, you will need to gather your materials and have your ducks in a row. Every teacher will tell you that when you're standing in front of the class explaining how to do an art lesson, and you suddenly remember you left the paper and paints in the Teacher's Lounge, then the afternoon will not go well. The same is true when the class is your own children, the classroom is the kitchen table, and the materials you need are on the top shelf of your closet. Preparing in advance means you will not have to scramble later. Set all the things you need where you can easily reach them before you need them. Chefs call it "mise en place," everything in its place, but you'll call it a lifesaver.

> *SIOBHAN'S STRATEGIES:* When I started homeschooling, I split up my schoolwork the way they had in school, with a small amount of each subject every day. I had my own shelf of a bookcase with my textbooks, notebooks, folders, and "done" tray, and I would get out what I needed for class, set up on the couch or at the table, and before I knew it I'd be done with that subject and have to go back to the bookcase to switch out my materials. The thing is that a 50-minute class minus the time it took to sit down, get my stuff out of my backpack, listen to the teacher read aloud (which takes longer than reading to oneself), wait after the teacher asked a question and no one volunteered to answer, sit through the teacher yelling at Taylor for be-

ing disruptive, etc. left me with only 15 minutes of actual coursework. I completely restructured my homeschooling organization to have one subject per day and to do a week's worth of work at a time. I still split up P.E., because doing 2 ½ hours of exercise once per week and none the rest of the week isn't healthy, and Art, because I feel a little creativity every day is good for the soul. If your school only needs a week's worth of assignments turned in once a week, there's no reason not to try splitting it up this way.

ORGANIZATIONAL MATERIALS

➤ *Calendars.* A calendar gives the big picture of where you are and where you're going. Find, buy, or make one big enough to write on. However you organize your homeschooling experience, put it on the calendar. It doesn't matter whether it's math every morning and reading every afternoon, or math on Monday, reading on Tuesday, and so on, as long as it's on the calendar. If you have field trips planned, either physical or virtual, seeing them on the calendar will give your kids something to look forward to. You can check off the days to mark the passage of time (which can be difficult to grasp if you're at home every day). Use sticky notes to add special events, and get creative. A sticky note with a picture of a pumpkin drawn by your child can signify a future trip to a pumpkin patch. Store-bought stickers can be a fun decoration, too. Make it personal, and checking the calendar won't be a chore.

➤ *Schedules.* Visual schedules are great! We all use them, don't we? Our phones and calendars are hand-held visual schedules that we rely on. Your child with ASD has probably used visual schedules in their classroom. Can you make one similar to the ones they've used before? Or come up with something that will catch their attention? What they need is to see at a glance what is in store for their day. Be sure to include fun things to anticipate as well as academic tasks.

> ***To Do & Done.*** This is a two-column list with things To Do on the left, which can be moved to the right column when they are Done. At school, they may have used laminated Tagboard, with Velcro buttons to stick picture icons of to-do tasks. Students could easily lift the task icon off the left side and stick it on the right side when the task was finished. If you don't have easy access to lamination and Velcro, replicate it with paper and sticky notes. Write or draw pictures of the to-do tasks and stick them all onto the left column at the beginning of the day in the order by which they should be done. As they finish the task, let your child pick up each sticky note and move it to the right column. It is satisfying to see the tasks moving from left to right as the jobs are completed! A much simpler idea is to just write a list and check off each item as it is finished. Moving a picture can be more engaging than just checking a box, but don't judge yourself if you don't have the time and energy to make a fancy chart. We're all doing the best we can, and that's good enough.

> ***Break it down.*** When there is a multi-step task that your child struggles with, break it down into baby steps. You might say "Get ready" and expect them to brush their teeth, wash their faces and hands, comb their hair, and put on their clothes, all on their own. How many times have you repeated yourself and sent them back to do the next step? Save yourself time and frustration by making separate "To Do & Done" charts or lists for the things you usually have to nag them about. Each step of "getting ready" would be a separate sticky note on the left side of their morning routine page, or a separate item on the list. If one of the steps is too complicated for them to easily remember, break it down even further: (1) put water on toothbrush, (2) take off toothpaste lid and set it down, (3) squeeze toothpaste on the brush, (4) brush all teeth: top, bottom, sides, front, back, (5) rinse mouth

with water and spit into sink, (6) rinse brush and put it in cup, (7) make sure the cap is back on the toothpaste, (8) wipe off any globs of toothpaste in or near the sink. Don't over-complicate things, though; if they regularly do a task independently, there's no need to create a chart for it. However, if you find yourself reminding your kids to do the same things every day, it's time to make a chart and let it do the reminding for you.

LEARNING MATERIALS

> *School Supplies.* Your child's school may supply you with some things, like textbooks, workbooks, or even an electronic tablet with assignments loaded onto it. You'll need to gather whatever they don't provide: pencils, pens, lined paper, etc. Just the basic things you'll find at Back-to-School sales. You don't need to invest in a lot of expensive classroom equipment. If you need maps, turn to the internet. It's not necessary to put up bulletin boards and alphabet wall charts or make your home look like a classroom, although if you want to, go for it. You can find storage solutions at stores that sell most items for around a dollar. Colorful bins for each subject plus a tray for finished work will make your child's workspace cheerful and organized.

> *Technology.* The internet is a wonderful teacher, if used prudently. Whatever subject your child is studying, there will be articles and videos galore. However, there are dangers. If you tell your child to do a search on a topic, it may accidentally lead to sites which range from slightly off-topic to downright disturbing. Prepare in advance by searching by yourself, then give your kids the links to sites you have pre-selected. Technology is an amazing tool, but use it wisely.

ENRICHMENT MATERIALS

➤ *Art Supplies.* Gather various arts and crafts materials into some more of those colorful bins you picked up at the around-a-dollar store. Crayons, colored pencils, sidewalk chalk, glue sticks, scissors, construction paper, tape, watercolors, markers—you can explore a different media every day. The secret is in having everything where you can organize and access it easily rather than scattered around their room or all muddled together in one big, miscellaneous "art box."

➤ *Building Materials.* There are lots of things kids can build with, and making something themselves is a valuable experience. Interlocking plastic bricks are great, especially if you have a range of colorful bricks with no specific directions. Let them get creative! (Just don't let them leave the bricks on the floor to be stepped on in the middle of the night!) Wooden blocks, building logs, gears and rods, popsicle sticks, even cardboard boxes—there are so many things your child can use to construct houses, cities, and universes of their choosing. Collect them into separate bins, and they will be at your fingertips when your child needs to take a break and build something.

Skip the last-minute scramble to find the things you need for a lesson. Getting set by gathering your materials in advance and making them easily accessible and organized is an important step toward being prepared for success.

CHAPTER 3: GO

Path to Success (You're Good to Go!)

"Even if you are on the right track, you'll get run over if you just sit there."
— Will Rogers

Y ou've gotten Ready to START Scheduling Theme-based Activities at Routine Times. You're Set for success with materials organized and prepared. Now it's time to Go forth on your path to homeschooling success. To get there, answer four W Questions: WHO, WHAT, WHERE, and WHEN.

WHO WILL BE PART OF YOUR HOMESCHOOLING TEAM?

➤ *Your Child* is obviously the most important one on the team. As much as possible and within reason, let them give input to guide their own homeschooling experience.

➤ *You* are your child's homeroom teacher now, creating and putting in place the educational experience you want for your child.

➤ *Your Family* is important to your homeschooling success. This includes the non-homeschooling spouse, if only one of you is taking on this role, siblings, and even extended family members important to your child's daily life.

➤ *Your Neighborhood School Staff.* If you are homeschooling in conjunction with your child's neighborhood school, be sure to use their resources. They are there to help all children learn, whether on-site or from home. They may provide books, materials, or online lessons.

➤ *Special Education Support Staff.* If your child has an Individualized Education Program (IEP), it is still valid while homeschooling. You will need to have a new IEP meeting, since home is a change of location. The IEP team will determine goals and services, resources they can provide for your child at home, and services you may be able to access by bringing your child to the school, such as those provided by the Speech and Language Pathologist (SLP) or the Occupational Therapist (OT). Some special services may be available via Telehealth.

WHAT WILL YOU TEACH?

> *Academics.* Your child's school can provide you with the standards that most children in their grade will be exposed to. Your child's IEP case manager can help you determine what is most important for your child to learn at this time. Focus on basic skills that will be most beneficial long-term. Knowing how to read for information, how to ask for help when needed, how to take care of basic self-help needs, and how to safely navigate the community and the internet are important. Knowing the capital of every state isn't really all that important for your child's future. As an adult, if we ever need to know a state capital for any reason, we can quickly search it from our smartphone. (That said, if your child has a passion for states and maps and loves memorizing such facts, it's fine to explore this during enrichment; just don't insist on it as an academic requirement.)

> *Social-Emotional.* Social-emotional education is always important, but when our planet is in the upheaval of a global pandemic, there are bound to be some very big feels. Allow emotional outlet rather than forcing cheerful optimism when they're not feeling it. While it's good to encourage looking on the bright side, don't push it until after you've accepted their honest expression of their negative feelings. Encourage them to draw and paint about their feelings, or write poetry or songs to share their emotions. They may miss their classmates if they are suddenly homeschooling due to school closures. Let them write letters and draw pictures, or make a memory book. Social

stories about COVID-19 can be helpful to process complex feelings. Even if they don't personally know anyone who has died, feeling grief is natural. The very concept that many people are afflicted by this terrible disease can be traumatic, and we shouldn't tell them these feelings aren't valid. After they know you have heard and understood their sad or anxious feelings, they may be ready to explore the upside to their current situation, and optimism may return.

➤ *Enrichment.* Beyond academics, there is a world of opportunities. Art, music, dance, drama, sculpting, building—all provide wonderful enrichment experiences. What can they make, what can they create, what can they learn, what questions can they get answered? Follow those trails of teachable moments!

WHERE WILL YOU TEACH?

➤ *At a dedicated workspace.* Your child will focus on academic tasks better if they have their own work area devoted to their homeschooling assignments. If they don't have a desk, small table, or folding tray to work on, designate a special place at the kitchen table. During homeschooling hours, show that it's for working rather than eating. Put out a special placemat that means work-time, and consider switching it out for a different placemat for lunchtime. If you don't have placemats, they can be bought cheaply, or your child can make some. Set out your child's organizational bins for books, materials, and the finished work tray, and display their visual schedule at their workspace.

➤ *Around the house.* The living room can become your school auditorium for viewing educational videos. The garage can be your science lab. Your backyard is your gym for P.E. As important as it is to have a special place to work, there's no need to spend the entire day sitting at a desk.

➤ *In the community.* When you can safely make trips around your community with your kids, do so. If masks are appropriate or mandated, make sure you have prepared your kids with social stories, and model proper mask-wearing behavior. Whether you are going to the grocery store (a great place for impromptu math and home economics lessons) or a museum, call first to see when it is least crowded. Outdoor places such as parks or local lakes and rivers are great enrichment experiences, as long as you can maintain social distance as needed.

➤ *Everywhere.* The internet opens up worlds that were not possible for previous generations. Want to go to a museum? How about the Louvre in Paris, or the Met in New York? Now you can visit them all, as well as zoos and aquariums and even outer space.

WHEN WILL YOU TEACH?

➤ *What is their best learning time?* Different people have different natural rhythms, and homeschooling provides a unique opportunity to embrace this. Maybe you're already aware of your child's best times, but it's all right to experiment in the early weeks of the school year to find their prime hours. Once you have a clear picture of their mental flow, you can get your schedule better adjusted to give your kids the best chance to succeed.

➤ *How long should you be teaching?* We spoke a little about how much time is "wasted" in traditional schooling. If your child is good at keeping their focus, they can probably complete a day's worth of academics in an hour or so for grade schoolers, or up to 3 ½ for older kids. If they're more distractible, you may want to break up the schoolwork into manageable chunks of time, say five minutes for a first grader or up to 15 minutes for a high schooler, with up to five-minute breaks in between.

➤ *Can you stagger learning schedules?* If you're like most of us, your home has approximately twice as many people as bathrooms. Your person-to-toaster ratio is probably even worse.

> **SIOBHAN'S STRATEGIES:** One of the best decisions I made in my homeschooling life was what I call Staggered Starts. I used to get up in the morning at around the time my siblings left for school. All the usual morning traffic jams at the bathroom and kitchen disappeared, and with them, a lot of stress left, too. Now, you'll most likely be teaching all your kids at home, so no one will be rushing out the door, but staggering your start times can still make a huge difference in reducing household stress and setting a good tone for the rest of the day. If you wake your kids as little as fifteen minutes apart, each kid will be the only one making breakfast, the only one brushing their teeth, and the only one getting set up at their desk at a given time. Some kids need more sleep than others, and unless your child's teacher scheduled an 8:00 AM Zoom, there's no reason they can't sleep in a little.

Now that you know Who is on your team, What you will teach, Where they will learn, and When their learning experiences will take place, it's time to start on your path to homeschooling success. You're good to go!

PART II

HAMMOCK:
Heart, Action, Mind, Music, Outdoors, Chores, Kitchen

"Variety's the very spice of life, that gives it all its flavour."
— *William Cowper*

What kinds of theme-based activities should you plan? To ensure a variety of experiences, plan activities around your HAMMOCK: Heart, Action, Mind, Music, Outdoors, Chores, and Kitchen. You can relax in your "hammock" while your kids explore the activities you have prepared for them. The next seven chapters dive into the various kinds of activities you can include for a well-rounded and balanced homeschooling experience.

CHAPTER 4: HEART

Activities That Speak to Kids' Feelings

"It is only with the heart that one can see rightly;
what is essential is invisible to the eye."
— Antoine de Saint-Exupery, *The Little Prince*

motions are a part of everyone's life, and it's important to recognize and honor the feelings in your child's heart. When a lot is going on around the globe and their personal world is a bit upside down, give them opportunities to express what is going on in their hearts. HEART activities do just that. What do we mean by HEART activities? Think of sparking MATCHES: Mindfulness, Art, Thankfulness, Charity, Helpfulness, Empathy, and Spirituality.

MINDFULNESS means being aware of and focused on the present moment rather than worrying about what happened in the past or what the future might hold. Practicing mindfulness is a great way to reduce stress, and we can all use that. Here are some activities that promote mindfulness:

> ➤ *Books.* There are a number of children's books about mindfulness. Lori Lite's picture book, *The Angry Octopus*, helps young kids use mindfulness to control angry outbursts. Dr. Raun Melmed and his associates have written several ST4 Mindfulness Books for Kids called the *Monster Diary* series. These are great for your children who are ready for chapter books. An internet search or trip to your local library's home page will probably turn up even more books about mindfulness for kids.

> ➤ *Sense Walks.* Each day, when you take a walk around your neighborhood, focus on a different sense. One day, have a *Sight Sense Walk*, where you notice the little things you might not have seen on other walks. What do you see that is your favorite color? Who can see the

tiniest thing? Who can see something high in the sky? Do you see neighborhood pets, or birds, or insects? Squirrel! How many petals does that flower have, and what does that cloud look like to you? Focusing on the sense of sight helps promote mindfulness. On another day, have a *Sound Sense Walk*, where you focus on what you can hear. As you become still and focus, you will notice many tiny sounds you may have been oblivious to before. Do you hear that insect buzz? The distant traffic, or sounds of water? A *Touch Sense Walk* will open up the differences between textures, the smoothness of a leaf, the roughness of the sidewalk. (You brought hand sanitizer, right? You'll need it.) Your *Smell Sense Walk* may run the gamut, from honeysuckle to car exhaust fumes to what you notice while cleaning up after your dog, but save the *Taste Sense Walk* for a walk around your kitchen.

➤ **Yoga.** Yoga is a great way to practice mindfulness. If you search "Yoga for Kids" or "Yoga for Autism," you will find many videos. Parents, watch them first and choose one that you think will be best for your family.

➤ **Meditation.** Meditation is another way to promote mindfulness. Being still may not be easy for your active kids, but it can be beneficial, either for focusing before starting work in the morning or for winding down at the end of a busy day. Watching flakes drift in a snow globe is calming and meditative. If you don't have a snow globe, you can make one from a jar and glitter (ask the internet how.) If your child is too old for naps but needs some quiet time each day to keep from bouncing off the walls, meditation may be just the thing.

ART is a great way to express what is in the heart. If you provide the materials, whether as simple as pencil and paper or as complicated as oil or acrylic paints on canvas, creating art is an essential Heart task. Here are a few ideas:

➤ *Still Life.* Arrange objects in an attractive way near a window or source of light and have your kids draw or paint it as they see it. Do this at least once a week. Consider having older kids take turns creating the still life for the whole family. Yes, parents can get in on this, too. It doesn't matter whether you're any good at drawing; when you join in and try art activities, you model for your child that creating art is important, that anyone can do it, and that it's not about skill; it's about heart.

➤ *Pounding Clay.* A lot of frustrations can be worked out while pounding clay or dough. If you don't have any, ask the internet how to make dough your child can play with. The cycle of creating and smashing and creating again can be therapeutic. Air-dry clay can be bought online or in craft and big box stores, and your child's creation can become a permanent sculpture without needing to be baked. Sensory sand, slime, and putty are all becoming more mainstream and available everywhere.

➤ *Found Art.* On your next walk, have your kids pick up bits of nature that catch their eye and heart. Leaves, twigs, pebbles—all can become art with some paper or cardboard, glue, and paint. Arranging items and photographing them can be an art project that doesn't require any supplies or wall space. Try photographing your arrangements with different filters or angles and talk about how it changes the mood of the finished piece.

➤ *Politics and Passions.* Some chalk and a sidewalk are all you need to let your kids express their feelings about whatever they are passionate about. It may be an issue in the news, it may be their frustration with COVID-19—whatever they want to write or draw about to show the world how they feel. Don't worry: if they go too far and write something that might offend the neighbors, a garden hose or a good rain will take care of it. However, do take pictures of their temporary art before the rainfall, so they will have a permanent record of their big feelings expressed in chalk.

➤ *Treasure Chest of Joy.* Find a box that's just the right size to hold in both hands. Let your child decorate it however they like with glitter, jewels, colors, feathers, whatever strikes their fancy. This will become their Treasure Chest of Joy. As an academic task, have them list things that make them happy. In the weeks before you make the box, you can spread this activity out over time by one day having them list things they can see that make them happy, another day things they hear that make them happy, and other days joy-producing things that they can smell, taste, or touch. Another time, have them go through the alphabet and see if they can think of something that makes them happy for each letter of the alphabet. What other prompts can you or your child think of to expand their list of things that bring them happiness? When they have compiled a good, long list, have them fill the box to turn it into their Treasure Chest of Joy. Try to find objects from their list that they can put in the box. For their favorite scent, put a few drops of extract, such as vanilla, lemon, or lavender, on a cotton ball in a resealable plastic bag. When they open the bag for a sniff, they can go to their happy place. If something is too big to fit in the box, have them draw a picture of it, or take a photo and print it to put in the box. Souvenirs from vacations that made them happy, ticket stubs, fidgets, reminders of fun times they've had with friends, anything that sparks joy in their hearts—put it in the box. Keep it where they can reach it anytime they feel down, so they can take out their Treasure Chest of Joy and explore it, refilling their capacity for happiness. Anytime you notice that they look sad, suggest a Treasure Chest break until they feel better. It warms the heart to see physical reminders of happy times and favorite things.

THANKFULNESS is an important Heart value. Having an attitude of gratitude has been shown to increase happiness. Here are some activities to nurture thankfulness in your child's heart:

> *Write a Note.* Writing is an academic standard you will need to address, so why not make a writing assignment that also promotes thankfulness? Who has done something nice for them? Let them write a thank-you note for that person. It can be a family member, a friend, or even a celebrity or community helper who's inspired them. Writing thank-you notes is a good way to improve academically while increasing the heart skill of thankfulness.

> *Make a Sign.* In these times, we have a lot of local heroes your family may want to thank, even if they don't know exactly whom they're thanking. Make a sign to put in your yard or window thanking your mail carrier, hospital heroes, or other essential workers.

> *Make a Video.* When they want to go beyond writing a simple thank-you note to someone special, let them make a video telling the person what they are grateful for, then send it to them. Grandparents love getting video thank-you messages from their grandkids! (Bonus: core curriculum requires presentations as part of Speaking and Listening standards. Your kids will be meeting educational standards and delighting their grandparents at the same time!)

> *Grow a "Compliment-Tree."* Make a "Compliment-Tree" out of a branch in a vase and cut out paper leaves. Family members can write complimentary messages for each other on the leaves and tape or tie them to the tree. This benefits the one who writes on the leaves as they focus on their gratitude and makes the recipient feel great about being appreciated and complimented.

> *Gratitude Journaling.* Sometimes it's difficult to find the good things in life when everything is hard. It feels like so much has been taken

from you. If you encourage your kids to write down 1-5 things they're grateful for every day, they can look back and realize how many good things still exist. Even if most of the things they write stay the same day to day (food, house, family), they'll still find something good about every day. As they get used to seeing the good in life, it'll get easier and easier to practice thankfulness.

> **SIOBHAN'S STRATEGIES:** Practicing thankfulness has been shown to improve symptoms of depression and anxiety. It would be a good idea to continue lighting these MATCHES even after the pandemic is over, when your family starts to navigate whatever the new normal will be.

CHARITY is a Heart activity that is perfectly suited to these times of sheltering at home. So many charities feed the hungry, provide protection for doctors and nurses, and help the homeless. You and your child may research charities and find one they would like to support, then brainstorm ways to support it. These may include:

➤ *Go Fund Them.* If there is a particularly worthy project, your child may wish to send them part of their allowance or earn extra money to donate. They might even start an online donation project to fund a cause. They will need parental supervision if this is the route they choose to take.

➤ *Make Masks.* There are still shortages of medical masks and other PPE around the world. If you have a sewing machine, maybe you can help your child learn to make masks to donate to local nursing homes or homeless shelters. There are lots of free patterns and tutorials online, and craft stores often have kits to get you started. Making masks is a great way to do something creative and helpful, and donating their work to help those in need may give them a feeling of control in a time when most things feel out of their control.

➤ *Post it, Share it.* Kids can make posts to support local or larger charity organizations to be shared on social media. Adult supervision is important, and parents should be the ones to actually post. Kids might want to raise awareness of a charitable organization or person and thank them for all the good work they're doing, expressing thankfulness and charity at the same time. After they make their awesome art, create posters, or even write poems in support of their favorite charity, their parents may post their thoughts online.

➤ *Little Free Sites:* Many neighborhoods are setting up "Little Free Libraries" and "Little Free Pantries" where people leave books or shelf-stable foods, respectively, for neighbors to take as needed. If your children have books they don't read anymore, they can donate them. Check your local area and social media; if you don't have a Little Free Library or Pantry near you, maybe you can start one.

HELPFULNESS is a Heart activity that is similar to Charity but closer to home. While charities help many people all over the world, being helpful is a family affair.

➤ *Notice it.* Invite everyone in the family to pay attention to helpfulness in the household. Who helped them today? Who did they help? Who did they see helping someone else? Raising awareness is an important first step to increasing helpfulness.

➤ *Stick it up.* Make a sticker chart, and every time someone notices another family member being helpful, they point it out, thank them, and put a sticker on the chart. It's best not to label the stickers or make columns for any particular person, which may promote competition and stress, but instead have a family goal to fill up the chart by everyone working together. You can even use your calendar, with the goal of having at least one helpfulness sticker per day. The opportunity to put a sticker on the chart encourages children to keep their eyes open and notice when others are being helpful.

➤ **Reward it.** When your family's helpfulness sticker chart is full of stickers, reward yourselves with a family fun activity. What do your kids love? Popcorn and a movie on the living room floor? Make-Your-Own-Sundae night? Create colorful frozen ice treats out of juice and fruit? Turn on the sprinklers and have everyone, even the parents, run through them? Let any special activity your kids enjoy be the family reward for practicing and noticing helpfulness.

EMPATHY is another Heart trait that can be strengthened. You may have heard others say that people on the autism spectrum lack empathy, but if you love and live with one, you probably recognize that as a myth. Sometimes our kids with ASD have unusual empathy, unexpressed empathy, or even exaggerated or heightened empathy. Even though they don't lack this Heart skill, any of us can benefit from increasing and expressing empathy. Activities include:

➤ **Someone Else's Shoes.** This is a game where family members try on each other's shoes. If the shoe doesn't fit, try it on a toe or finger or thumb, or wear it on your head. While wearing that person's shoes, try to view the world through their eyes. Share what you think the other person might be feeling or thinking. Ask the person if you are on the right track or way off base.

➤ **Freaky Friday.** This game is based on the movie with the same name. Two family members, usually a parent and a child, pretend to be each other. Everyone calls them by the other's name for the duration of the game. They wear articles of that person's clothing, and say and do what they think the other person would say or do. It's a fun step beyond Someone Else's Shoes.

➤ **Books.** When reading aloud to your children at bedtime, encourage empathy by asking how they think the character might feel. What are the clues that let you know about their inner thoughts? Discussing others' feelings is a good way to increase empathy.

➤ *The TV Game.* While watching a movie or television show, press pause and ask how the person on the screen might be feeling at that moment. Why do you think they feel that way? How can you tell? It's important to set this up in advance as a game that involves pausing the show, to avoid the upset of being interrupted. Also, don't choose anyone's favorite show for this, and don't play if someone hasn't seen that episode before. In addition, having kids take turns being the one to press pause and ask the question puts power in their hands.

SPIRITUALITY is an important Heart component. Whether or not your family has a particular faith, the pandemic is a time when you can focus on your personal beliefs and values, such as equality, integrity, justice, having each other's back, or sticking up for the underdog. If you're used to worshiping in a church or temple, in addition to joining online services, let your child help plan a service at home. If you have moved and they miss their old church family, now you can join online worship services anywhere around the globe. You don't have to be a member of any religion to grow spiritually in your own way. Sharing your personal spiritual path with your children helps them develop their own spirituality.

Homeschooling is a wonderful opportunity to focus on the heart, express emotions, and spark MATCHES with Mindfulness, Art, Thankfulness, Charity, Helpfulness, Empathy and Spirituality. Focusing on these things can decrease stress and increase feelings of peace and happiness. Isn't that what we all need right now?

CHAPTER 5: ACTION

Activities That Get Kids Moving

"Human beings must have action; and they will make it if they cannot find it."

— George Eliot

B eing physically active has been shown to be effective against anxiety and depression, and even beneficial with sleep problems. When they aren't in school, your children don't have recess time or P.E. to go outside and get moving every day. However, you can schedule P.E. at home and provide them with a list of activities they can choose from. Think WILD when you think of action: Walkabout, Imitate, Lift, and Dance.

> ➤ *Walkabout.* Take a trip around your neighborhood or cruise the perimeter of a local park or playground on your Walkabout. You don't have to walk; you can jog, speed walk, run, or even bike or scooter. Your dog will love coming along for the fun!

> ➤ *Imitate.* How many animals can your kids imitate? Swinging their arm like an elephant's trunk? Slithering on the floor like a snake? Jumping like a kangaroo? Side-walking like a crab? Let them help you come up with more animals to imitate. Older kids can be leaders and have younger kids imitate them in doing jumping jacks, squats, or whatever exercise routine they come up with.

> ➤ *Lift.* When lifting, think in terms of strength training to improve health, not weightlifting to build muscle mass. Don't start a weightlifting routine for your child or teen without consulting a professional and their doctor. There are many healthy strength training activities your kids can safely do right now. Lifting groceries out of the bag and putting them on the shelves is helpful as well as health-promoting. Lifting wet laundry from the washer and putting it into the dryer is

another one. What can your kids think of that would be fun for them? Lifting stuffed animals over their head while dancing? Lifting books or canned goods? Seeing who in your family can hold a plank the longest? All of these are examples of healthful action.

➤ *Dance.* Having a regularly scheduled Family Dance Night is a fun idea. Your kids will love it if you join them in dancing like no one's watching. Kids can collaborate on the playlist, then rock out! Or, host a "silent rave" where everyone picks their own tunes on headphones. Make it even more festive by dimming the lights (not too dark, safety first) and shining a flashlight on a disco ball or other reflective object. In addition to the Dance Night on the calendar, surprise them once in a while with Random Dancing! If your kids start to feel that homeschooling is boring or monotonous, jump out and yell, "EVERYBODY DANCE!" Crank it up and cut loose for one song. That'll shake things up!

There are plenty of wild ways you can get your kids to be more active. When they do, consider downloading an app of cheering sounds on your phone and playing it whenever they finish an active task. Then let them raise their fists, Rocky-style, and bask in the applause.

> **SIOBHAN'S STRATEGIES:** Different exercises are good for different times of day. First thing in the morning, you may need to get the family up and active to start the day. Get the blood pumping! Midday, you may want your kids to work up an appetite for lunch. In the evenings, when school is done and you need everyone to start winding down for bed, relaxing yoga might help everyone stretch out and feel calm together.

CHAPTER 6: MIND

Activities That Get Kids Thinking

"The mind is not a vessel to be filled but a fire to be kindled."

— Plutarch

Your child's teacher has probably provided schoolwork to be done at home. Any school task will give your child's mind a workout, including math or spelling flashcards, worksheets, chapter questions in textbooks, or exploring their own interests through reading or on the internet. But there's a lot more to learning than meets the eye, and there are many paths to improving the mind.

MIX IT UP, MAKE IT FUN.

➤ *Alternate worksheets or assignments* from school with more active or preferred learning experiences. You can alternate between doing a few math problems and writing a sentence using a spelling word, if your child craves variety and hates to be tied down to a paper until it is finished.

➤ *Time it!* How quickly do they think they can finish that assignment? For kids who have trouble getting started on a task but enjoy a challenge, pulling out your phone's stopwatch can get them moving. Be aware, though, that for some kids this is stressful, not fun. Pay attention to your child's nonverbal messages when you mention timing them. Do they look anxious, fearful, or upset? Then you can say, "Never mind, we don't have to time it. You do it at your own speed." Your kids who love the timer may start asking you to time everything they do, from brushing their teeth to putting away their clean clothes. It's okay to use a strategy for one child but not the others, based on their unique personalities. That's what individualization is all about, and homeschooling is the perfect place to let each child learn in their own way.

> ➤ **Break it down.** If that math paper looks too overwhelming, make a game of it. First, trim it down to 6 or 12 problems, depending on how much you feel your child can tolerate. Remember that we are all under a lot of stress right now, whether it shows or not. For your child, this may mean being unable to complete a full page of math that they could do easily a few months ago. Even if you do only 6 of the problems on the page, your child will have had a mathematical academic experience. Don't try to do 26 problems if your child becomes overwhelmed at the sight and either freezes or acts out in frustration. Better to have fun doing 6 problems by making it a game.

> ➤ **Random Roll.** Here's how to play the game:
> 1. Cut the math paper and put away the rest so your child only sees 6 (or 12) problems.
> 2. Give your child a six-sided die (or two dice if you're doing 12 problems).
> 3. Have them roll the die/dice.
> 4. Whatever number they roll, they complete that problem. If they roll a three, they do problem #3 on the page.
> 5. Roll again, and keep rolling until the paper is finished.
> 6. If they roll a repeat number, meaning they've already done that problem, decide in advance what to do. Consider one of these ideas or whatever your child thinks would be fun:
>   a. Check that problem using a calculator and correct it if needed.
>   b. Raise their fists and chant, "I already did it! I'm awesome!"
>   c. Run a lap around the room while playing cheers on an applause app.
>   d. All of the above if they need longer breaks sprinkled throughout the task.

ACE ACADEMICS

You can help your child ACE their academics by alternating Assigned tasks, Chosen tasks, and Extra tasks.

> *Assigned tasks.* There will always be assigned tasks that must be done. Kids need to know which things are optional and which are required. They may not need to do the required tasks all at once. Stagger assigned tasks with tasks they chose and extra enrichment tasks to keep it interesting.

> *Chosen tasks.* These are tasks your kids can choose for themselves. Do they want to read the grade-level literature book themselves, have you read to them, take turns every other page or chapter, or follow along while listening to the audiobook? They choose. Try to increase the number and type of activities that they may choose for themselves to get more buy-in.

> *Extra tasks.* If they finish all of their assignments quickly but you're not ready for them to have the rest of the day as free play, make a list of extra, fun things they may choose to do. Extra P.E. activities? Arts and crafts? Internet exploration and enrichment? Make a chart of what they can do when they finish early. Get their input about what should be on the chart, and they will be more likely to have fun with it.

TRIPLE EX ENRICHMENT

Enrich your child's learning experience by letting them eXamine, eXpand, and eXplore topics that spark their curiosity and interest.

> *Examine.* Sometimes a topic is barely mentioned in a science, history, or other textbook, but it captures your kid's imagination, and they want to learn all about it. What causes earthquakes? Why do birds migrate? Are butterfly wings like fish scales when you look at them

under a microscope? Give them the freedom to examine the topics they're interested in.

> *Expand.* Starting with the subjects they want to examine more closely, expand that interest into related subjects. If today is Mountain Day in Japan, after learning about mountains, what can you learn about Japan? Does an interest in Fujiyama lead to speculation about volcanoes? Or learning Japanese words, making sushi, or reading manga? Let one interest expand into another. It's not off-task; it's all learning.

> *Explore.* The topics that are most interesting to your child and that fuel their passions can be explored more deeply. The internet or your library can offer a wealth of information on the subjects your child wants to dive into. Exploring opens the mind, and learning takes off!

SIOBHAN'S STRATEGIES: Maybe your family can make a time capsule of your time sheltering at home. When I was learning about World War II, my grandmother showed me a box of things she had saved from her childhood. I got to see the ration booklets, ticket stubs from charity cake walks, and even her sister's old makeup case. Did you know that when stockings were unavailable, girls would put makeup on their legs? She told me about how her older sister would stand on a chair while my grandmother drew seam lines down the backs of her legs with eyebrow pencil. What little things can you save away for your kids to show their grandkids someday about the age of coronavirus?

You can support your child in developing their thinking skills and watch them grow to love learning. First, mix it up and make it fun, alternating tasks, breaking down long assignments into chunks, and making a game of it. Help them ACE academics with assigned tasks, chosen tasks, and extra tasks. Finally, dive deeply into enrichment by examining, expanding, and exploring their passions. Set them up to enjoy exercising their minds now, and you will create life-long learners when they grow up.

CHAPTER 7: MUSIC

Activities That Sing

"Music is the universal language of mankind."

— Henry Wadsworth Longfellow

Incorporating music throughout the day can relieve stress. Playing classical music in the background while working can be calming for many, and some studies suggest it improves grades. Other kids will want to replay their favorite songs again and again and again. Don't be impatient with this; during difficult times, repetition can be enormously comforting. Do you have a playlist that cheers you up when you're down or settles you when you're upset? Music is a great way to process and express feelings, for us and for our children.

Of course, if you have real musical instruments and sheet music in the house, music-making might be easy, but don't think a lack of equipment or instruction means your family must miss out on the magic of music.

When you think of MUSIC, think Movement, Uplifting, Sing-along, Imagine, Create.

> ➤ *Movement.* Remember when your child was a toddler, how they would bounce and sway whenever you put on their favorite music? They're not too old to get that same exhilaration from moving to music. Maybe your child wants to learn the latest dance craze from social media. Try learning it with them, or just be their camera operator and post the result. Not their style? It doesn't have to include any real dance steps, as long as they keep moving when the music starts. You can play Musical-Chairs-Meets-Statues without the chairs. As long as the music plays, everybody moves, and as soon as it stops, everyone freezes. Try to come up with interesting frozen tableaux, and snap a picture. Let kids take turns being in charge of starting and stopping

the music, and taking the photo from their chosen angle and using whatever filters or stickers they like.

> **Uplifting.** Music can be particularly uplifting, especially in times of troubles. Listening to virtual choirs with each member singing from their own home can be inspiring, and watching as one after another singer is added and the music swells can be awe-inspiring. If you attend virtual church services, then listening to your familiar choir, even virtually, may be uplifting for you. Ask your kids what kinds of music make them feel this way. Classical instrumentals? A song that is awesome, one that gets stuck inside their head? Bagpipes or jug bands? Whatever music lifts your kids up, be sure to include it in their homeschooling days.

> **Sing-along.** Get the whole family involved in a sing-along or karaoke. You can find the songs you love with lyrics printed out in online videos. Let each person who wants to take the spotlight have a solo, then get everyone on stage for a big production number. If you have a budding choreographer in the family, let them direct, then set up a phone to record the whole thing. You'll have fun watching it and singing along with yourselves for years to come.

> **Imagine.** Music can spark the imagination in so many ways. Let your kids lean back and close their eyes while you play Grieg's *In the Hall of the Mountain King* or Tchaikovsky's *Dance of the Sugarplum Fairy*. What images play behind their eyelids? Then let them draw, dance, or write a poem about what they imagined. Keep playing the music while they express themselves.

> **Create.** Did you know your house is full of musical instruments? I'll bet your kids do, or at least they did when they were two. Remember pot lid symphonies? What about the music of squeaking door hinges, crumpling paper bags, tapping and clapping, playing spoons, or pulling a straw up and down in a takeout cup lid? Have your kids put

together an orchestra of found or created instruments and put on a show for your listening pleasure. They are giving their brain an imagination workout while creating unexpected music.

> **SIOBHAN'S STRATEGIES:** Have you ever been watching a movie or show and found yourself saying, "Wow, that's a great song choice"? Music can completely change the mood of a scene. It can also change the mood of the homeschool classroom. Work with your kids to make a playlist that really motivates them, calms them, or cheers them up. Make it your classroom soundtrack! If the kids can't agree, separate playlists and headphones will be necessary. Listening to the same music each time they crack open the books will help them build a routine and get into the right mindset for learning.

You and your kids will probably come up with many more ways to make music a part of your daily homeschooling experience, through rhythmic movement, uplifting songs, family sing-alongs, imagining to music, and creating their own instruments and musical pieces. Enjoy your musical family!

CHAPTER 8: OUTDOORS

Activities That Get Kids Out of the House

"I go to nature every day for inspiration in the day's work."

— Frank Lloyd Wright

J ust because you're sheltering at home doesn't mean you need to stay inside all the time. Follow the regulations in your area; most communities allow walking around your neighborhood or visiting parks that remain open. Just remember to practice safe physical distancing if you see other people, and never go out without your masks. If you have a yard, you have the perfect place to get some sunshine and fresh air, so get out and breathe … and when I say breathe, I mean BREATHE: Bike, Run, Explore, Attune to nature, Try something new, Hunt scavenger-style, and Examine tiny things.

> ➤ **Bike.** This is a great time to get the bikes out, oil them up, check the tires, and set off on a family bike ride. Don't have bikes? Affordable ones are often found in thrift stores or in the classifieds. You may even find bike or scooter rentals in your city. Remember to review safety regulations on riding bikes in your community, and put on that helmet before you head out. Don't want bikes? How about scooters? Skateboards? Roller skates? Pogo sticks? Anything that gets the kids outdoors and moving is a good idea. If you don't have any of these, just get out and run.

> ➤ **Run.** While being mindful of traffic and safety concerns, running is a great form of exercise, in moderation as with everything. Jogging, relay racing, speed walking, or even strolling along at an easy pace are all ways to get the benefits of the great outdoors. Look both ways!

> ➤ **Explore.** Check out your neighborhood. Pull up a map on your phone and expand it to see what is near you, and farther out. Are there any

parks on the map that you haven't been to? Make a date on your calendar for an adventure! A river, lake, or pond nearby? Go exploring! You can even go on a car expedition by letting your kids choose which way to turn at every corner. Right or left? Who knows what you'll find by the time you're done turning this way and that? If you go too far afield, use your phone's GPS or a map to find your way back home again. That's a local geography lesson right there!

➤ *Attune to nature.* Some kids love to hug trees, literally. Their love of nature is so great that they can hardly contain it. When their world gets stressful, returning to nature and attuning to it can return them to harmony. Next time things get crazy around the house, consider going out to a park or open place, as far as possible from the sounds of traffic, and just sit. Listen. Be in nature. It can be a healing experience.

➤ *Try something new.* Be adventurous! Never ridden a tandem bicycle built for two? See if you can rent one in your neighborhood. Never visited a nearby carousel? Maybe today is the day. Have your kids ever decorated your driveway or sidewalk with chalk? Let them! What else can you do outdoors that's new to you? Expand your horizons.

➤ *Hunt, scavenger-style.* Create scavenger hunt lists for a variety of settings, such as in the backyard, in a park, or on a drive. While driving, have them look for things such as a yellow car, a dog, a billboard with a picture of food, a stoplight with an arrow on it, a traffic sign shaped like a diamond, and so on. In your backyard or a park, have them look for things like a tiny flower, a long stick, a leaf with points, and a round stone. Let older kids create scavenger hunt lists for younger kids. If they have access to a phone, consider including things on the list that they can photograph but not actually pick up, such as a bird, a cloud shaped like an animal, a ladybug, or a tall tree. If you can pair an adult or teen with each younger child, they can team up, with the younger one being the lookout to find things, and the older team member reading the list and taking the pictures. Later, at home, everyone can share what they found. Another kind of hunt is an Easter-egg-style hunt, only it doesn't have to be at Easter, and you don't even need to use eggs. All you need is a number of similar objects, such as toddler-sized plastic building bricks or blocks or various kinds of balls. You can hide them first, then let the kids take turns hiding them and finding them. They'll get plenty of fresh air and sunshine, and they'll have a ball!

➤ **Examine tiny things.** It can be fascinating to look at very small things. Does your child love to watch ants walking in a line, carrying bits of food bigger than they are? Do they examine grains of sand to notice the many different colors and shapes? For once, let them spend as much time as they want to in these outdoor pursuits. If you have a magnifying glass, that's even better, but stick to shady areas so the sun being magnified through it can't start any tiny fires. Unless that's the lesson you're teaching under adult supervision. Safety first!

> *SIOBHAN'S STRATEGIES:* Homeschooling doesn't mean you have to keep school in the home. You can easily bring your book or tablet outside and do your reading on the porch. Need some quiet? Your teen can make the passenger seat their classroom and study while you're running errands. Your local park might be taking reservations at the picnic tables. If your kids like audiobooks, they can listen while you're on your family walk as long as they remember safety rules. Sometimes, when you're always in the house, any other space becomes inspiring!

No matter what Outdoor time looks like for your family, enjoy it together. We all spend enough time inside our homes these days. Any time we can get out and soak up some rays or dodge some raindrops is time well spent. And remember to BREATHE.

CHAPTER 9: CHORES

Activities That Get the Job Done

"Some people regard discipline as a chore.
For me, it is a kind of order that sets me free to fly."

— Julie Andrews

N obody likes chores, but they must be done, so let's make them fun. Maybe your family was fortunate enough to hire someone to do the major household jobs in your house, but since the pandemic they may not be available, or you may have cut back for financial concerns. Maybe the parents have always done the housework, but now you realize your kids are capable of pitching in. Even very young children can do simple chores, like putting away clean spoons from the dishwasher or matching socks from the dryer. Starting young, when they are excited to help out, will help when they are older. You will have established a routine of helping out, which leads to good work ethics. The time to start that routine is now, and here's how: When you think about chores, think WORK: Weekly chores, Once-a-day chores, Reinforce it, and Keep it professional.

> **Weekly chores.** Make a list of all of the chores that must be done weekly to keep your household running smoothly. Now, look at your list and decide if there are any jobs that require an adult, such as laundry that includes delicates or items which could easily be ruined, or working with chemical cleaning products. Next, find jobs that may be done by a teen, such as vacuuming and mopping or cleaning the kitchen. Look for jobs that are simple enough for everyone, so that even your youngest children can do them, like dusting surfaces with no breakable objects or putting away groceries. Mark each item E for Everyone, T for Teens, or A for Adults. (Of course, if you don't have teens in your household, those jobs would revert to parents, and all tasks would be either E or A.) Weekly chores may be above and be-

yond their usual routine, and children should be reinforced for taking on a big job.

➤ *Once-a-day chores.* There are jobs that must be done daily, such as making beds, picking up toys from the living room, putting dirty dishes into the dishwasher, and emptying the dishwasher and putting away the clean dishes. These may also be labeled for Everyone, Teens or Adults. Often, these jobs are expected with no remuneration and seen as their contribution to keeping the family running smoothly.

➤ *Reinforce it.* We all expect to be paid when we have a job, and kids are no different. Of course, you may assign regular chores that everyone does just because they are part of the family. It's wise to instill the idea that we are all in this household together and we all contribute to making it work without expecting payment. You reinforce these chores by acknowledging how they have helped the family and by praising their hard work. When there are additional chores you'd like the kids to do beyond the usual ones, be willing to pay for the extra work. Their payment may be in money or in extra privileges. Just let them know in advance what reinforcement they're working for. It's smart to get their input. Would they rather have extra screen time, the chance to play with your video game system, a special solo trip to the park with a parent and no siblings, a particular toy they've been wishing for, or cold, hard cash? They will work harder to earn something that is meaningful to them.

➤ *Keep it professional.* When you are professional about their work, they learn valuable job skills they will need in the future. Rather than assigning chores like a parent, let them apply for the jobs they want, like a boss. Create a Help Needed bulletin board and put it on the refrigerator. Post the jobs you want done and how much you're willing to pay for each one. Make sure the payment is in line with the job difficulty and that you are offering something they value. If you offer them a dollar to clean the garage, you may not get any applicants. On the other hand, if you offer $25.00 to do a load of laundry, you could go broke while they develop unrealistic expectations. Once you have determined the jobs and their worth, let the kids go through the job-seeking process. Be fair, though. If more than one kid wants the same job, make it a temp position for a week or month, then re-post it and interview again so someone else has the opportunity. Here are the steps:

1. *Apply.* Have them fill out an application form you create. If you have older kids or teens, let them make one for you. Consider requiring a written letter of application or essay about why they would be the best person for the job. They will be fulfilling a written language task while learning employability skills.

2. *Interview.* Everyone should take the interview process seriously, dressing for success and looking their best. The interview panel may be one or two parents. Prepare at least three questions in advance, such as "Why do you want this position?" "What are your strengths and weaknesses?" and "Are you capable of doing the job?"

3. *Work.* There must be accountability, such as a checklist of the parts of the job. You've seen this kind of thing in public restrooms where they have a clipboard that employees check and initial with the day and time each task was completed. Having a broken-down task list for each job helps promote success.

4. *Get paid.* Whatever you agreed on, be sure to pay up promptly. No one wants to wonder when they're getting paid for their work, so be as professional an employer as you want them to be as employees.

SIOBHAN'S STRATEGIES: Prioritize the chores realistically. Having the table cleared of schoolwork before dinner? High priority. Beds made before breakfast? Or at all? Low priority. Not everything is going to get done every day or week. It's okay to fall a little behind; just focus on getting the most important chores taken care of.

Remember to WORK with Weekly chores and Once-a-day chores, and to Reinforce it and Keep it professional. Be creative about how you pay your children for extra chores, keeping in mind their personal passions and preferences. One child may want to earn money toward purchasing a small trampoline, and another might be happy to earn the privilege of choosing what's for dessert tonight or helping cook it. Speaking of cooking …

CHAPTER 10: KITCHEN

Activities That Put Food on the Table

"Everything happens in the kitchen. Life happens in the kitchen."
— Chef Andrew Zimmern

Having kids in the kitchen is a recipe for fun as well as learning. Depending on their age and responsibility, you will need to be more or less involved, especially around knives and heat sources, but let your children take on as much of the cooking as they are safely able to do. They will have fun while they learn, and you all get to enjoy the fruits of their labors. When coming up with kitchen activities, think like a CHEF: Cook, Harvest, Eat, and Feed the family.

> ➤ ***Cook.*** Cooking not only is an important life skill, but also supports academics. Children read recipes, follow multi-step directions, and use math to measure ingredients. When they cook alongside other family members on a team, it promotes social skills. Since everybody eats, knowing how to cook is vital to survival. Plus, it's fun! Whether they're getting up to their elbows in flour while kneading dough, decorating cookies for Christmas gifts, or choosing a rainbow of veggies and fruits for an after-supper TV snack, your kids will love their time in the kitchen!

> ➤ ***Harvest.*** If you're fortunate enough to have a garden plot, lucky you! Let your kids help decide what they would like to grow in the garden. Harvesting your own radishes or zucchini or tomatoes is quite an accomplishment! If you don't have a garden outside, consider a kitchen garden to grow herbs they can harvest to add to any meal. You might grow your own sprouts for salads in a mason jar on the windowsill. Regrowing vegetables is another fun experience. While you may never harvest a whole carrot from the cut-off end, if you put it in

a small dish of water, you can enjoy watching the carrot greens shoot up. If you put the root end of a head of lettuce in a dish of water, you won't get a full-sized head of lettuce, but you will be able to harvest a few leaves for a sandwich or small salad. Have you ever tried storing scallions in a vase of water like a straight-up green bouquet and snipping the tops of the greens for garnish as needed? Your kids will love growing and harvesting their own contributions to the dinner table!

> *Eat.* Do you have a picky eater at home? Many kids on the spectrum have self-limited diets, sometimes due to food textures, colors, taste, or simply unfamiliarity and resistance to trying something different. If you want your kids to branch out of their food comfort zone, let them prepare new foods for dinner. They may be more willing to give it a taste when they've been working with it before it reaches their plate. Increasing familiarity with new foods by preparing them can lead to expanding what they are willing to try.

> *Feed.* When your kids feed the family by preparing a meal for everyone, their personal sense of accomplishment and self-worth can skyrocket! Receiving thanks and praise from their parents and siblings means so much. We all feel good about ourselves when we contribute to others; it's a human thing, and your children will benefit as much from feeding others as from feeding themselves.

SIOBHAN'S STRATEGIES: Does anyone in your family have a favorite cooking show? Why not pretend to host an episode in your kitchen? Maybe you'll all need to come up with different ways to use a secret ingredient, or put random back-of-the-pantry items in a basket to make a surprise meal (maybe some of those weird substitutions the grocery app gave you?) or challenge them to make a dish where all the ingredients start with the same letter. Everyone has to call each other "Chef" while cooking and judging, and nobody judges a dish they refuse to taste (it's okay to taste and discreetly spit out if something really isn't edible.) When judging, practice social skills by offering constructive criticism and accepting judgment with grace and patience. Expand vocabulary skills by outlawing certain words, like "gross," and making more specific vocabulary choices. If you want to, you can film and edit your food show for the grandparents!

Of all the activities you can do with your children during homeschooling, cooking with them probably adds the most value. You are teaching them life skills, social skills, and academics, and improving the quality of their future life by expanding their horizons and increasing their ultimate independence. What a gift!

PART III

ACT:
Activities that Create
Teachable moments

"The quality of life is determined by its activities."
— *Aristotle*

CHAPTER 11: VARIED

Vote, Alternate, Recharge, Improvise, Empower, Dare

> "Take an object. Do something to it. Do something else to it.
> Do something else to it."
>
> — Jasper Johns, artist

Everything educates. Children, especially, are designed to learn all the time, not just during school. We often use the term "teachable moments" to describe learning opportunities that come up in everyday life. If you want to create teachable moments that your kids will respond to, avoid getting into a rut. Of course, predictability and routine are important to your students on the spectrum, but within those familiar structures, surprise them with activities that are VARIED: Vote, Alternate, Recharge, Improvise, Empower, and Dare.

> ➤ **Vote.** All kids enjoy wielding a certain amount of power, and our kids on the spectrum often have a greater need for control than their siblings do. During uncertain times, that need can loom large as children try to control everything, from what they will eat or wear to when or where they will go to the bathroom. When a child cannot control much, they make the most of the few things they can. If you let the family vote on decisions that affect everyone, you make sure every voice gets heard. Especially during an election year, voting in the homeschool classroom creates teachable moments about democracy and decision-making. Every once in a while, find an issue that you're willing to accept two outcomes to, and put it up for a vote. Be on the lookout for potential problems at the polling place. Don't let siblings "gang up" on each another or try to coerce others to vote with them. That kind of pressure is not allowed in the voting booth,

and it shouldn't be allowed in the home. Consider a secret ballot to avoid problems. And, of course, don't put anything on the ballot that you wouldn't be willing to live with. It's not okay to let them vote then overrule their decision because their choice is inconvenient for you. Let the vote stand.

> *Alternate.* Switch up their schedules, alternating when they have certain subjects or routines. Consider having a Schedule A and Schedule B, and alternating them every other week or month. Observe how your kids respond to each schedule. If one of them seems to result in more challenging behavior and less productivity, take it off the table and try something different. Ask your kids how they feel about various schedules. Alternate their old routines with new ones that are also predictable but different to keep things fresh without losing the security of the familiar.

> *Recharge.* Some days will be hard. News will be bad. Weather will be uncomfortable. Everything that might go wrong seems to spiral downward. You need to recharge your batteries. Perhaps your literature lesson could be replaced by listening to the audiobook while relaxing on the rug, eyes closed, breathing mindfully. We're not really sure why people put cucumber slices on their eyes, but maybe this is an occasion for such a thing. Or perhaps you need to recharge in a more active way. Count by fives while jumping rope, one number for each jump. Spell vocabulary words while upside down on the couch, feet in the air. What recharges your batteries? Whatever works for you and your kids, use it to create teachable moments.

> *Improvise.* As much as we all love a schedule, there may be times when we need to toss it. (Don't really toss it; you'll need that tomorrow!) Tell your kids that you will be improvising for one day. Have them give you math problems to solve for a change. (They will need to check if you were correct, of course.) Instead of reading another

chapter in your literature book, have them act out what they think the characters might do next, then read ahead and see if they were on track. Play a game of *Whose Line Is It Anyway?* and have kids make up and act out scenes based on words the audience (you) throws at them. If the words happen to be vocabulary from their history lesson, you have created a teachable moment and tons of fun at the same time.

➤ *Empower.* Like we said, kids love power. When do kids get to be king? When you empower them. Consider having a knighting ceremony to dub your child Sir Chooses Dessert or Lady Remote Control for a day. Let them make decisions within their scope of knighthood, all day long. They can even give you ideas of what they would like to be empowered to do. Of course, their power is limited. They can't drive the car without a license or declare a holiday from their parents' work to go to Disneyland. But, what are you willing to empower them to do? And how will they wield their new power? With kindness and compassion? This can be an important teachable moment as well as a fun way for your child to feel empowered.

➤ *Dare.* Dare them to do something different. Never ridden a bike before? I dare you! Never written a poem, tasted broccoli, or done five math problems in five minutes? Dare you to try! A dare can be a teachable moment when you invite them to stretch their previous limits and see what they are truly capable of achieving. And it's fun! Be ready, though, for what they might dare you to try. (A warning: the Double-Dog Dare is a powerful tool and should not be used except in extreme cases. We advise against it. The traditional single dare is usually sufficient for the purpose of the teachable moment.)

New activities can keep homeschooling fresh, ward off boredom when you can't get out, and create a wealth of teachable moments. Keep your days VARIED by letting your kids Vote, Alternating schedules, Recharging your batteries, Improvising instead of sticking to a script,

Empowering your kids to make more decisions themselves, and Daring them to try something new. If you keep your eyes open, teachable moments will appear in unexpected places!

> **SIOBHAN'S STRATEGIES:** Teachable moments can come from anywhere. Think about a place and time your kids are learning about in history and find a related (age-appropriate) movie. Make food from that region for dinner and have a themed night! If one of your kids is taking French, you can watch the movie *Ratatouille* and make ratatouille for dinner. If they're studying Native American cultures, watch *Brother Bear* and make salmon for dinner. Third graders who read *James and the Giant Peach* can watch the movie and help make peach pie for dessert. If they're studying insects in science, watch *A Bug's Life* and make honey buns. (Feeling brave? Order edible crickets from the internet.)

CHAPTER 12: FUN ACTIVITIES

Frequent, Unscheduled, New

"If you never did, you should. These things are fun, and fun is good."

— Dr. Seuss

E ven though you provide a variety of activities to address the lessons and skills you need to introduce during homeschooling, don't forget to toss in a few things just for fun. Pencil in new games and unscheduled breaks frequently with activities that promote laughter and silliness. Speaking of silliness, since these activities are not in the START category of Scheduling Theme-based Activities at Routine Times, consider calling them FART activities: Fun Activities at Random Times. After one of these short breaks from work, your kids may be in a better mood and more focused on learning. In any case, your job as a parent includes keeping your child safe and happy. Here are some FUN activities that are Frequent, Unscheduled, and New.

> *Frequent.* Make these silliness breaks a frequent addition to your daily work schedule, within reason. If they are too frequent, several times a day, they will eat up too much of your work time. Not only that, your kids may come to expect that homeschooling is more a party than a learning experience. On the other hand, if the fun breaks are too far apart, your kids may become bored with the regular routine. You know your children. Observe them for signs of screen fatigue, boredom, or impatience. That is the time to jump up, shout "FART!" and pull a FUN activity out of your hat. (If you actually keep slips of paper with FARTs in a hat, that would be fun!)

> *Unscheduled.* These FART activities will be unscheduled as far as your kids are concerned, but you can schedule them on your private calendar. If your kids live by their visual schedule, make a sticky note

or Velcro icon with the word "SURPRISE!" or "FART!" and stick it on the schedule as soon as you declare it. Then enjoy the fun!

➤ *New.* Make up new activities that everyone can enjoy. (Just remember, if it's not fun for everybody, it's not really fun. Keep an eye open to see if one child finds a new activity too stressful, and modify accordingly.) Put as many fun ideas as you can think of in your FART hat so your kids won't get tired of the same old, same old. Here are some ideas to get you started:

- *Random Dance Party!* Turn on a favorite song, shout "FART! Random Dance Party!" and start rocking out! Everyone puts down their pencils and dances until the music ends!

- *Mad Tea Party Switcheroo!* If all of your kids are seated at a table, this FART makes everyone stand up and move to the next chair. (Do not use this if any of your kids are particularly attached to their special chair.)

- *Opera Moment!* Everyone takes turns standing and singing at the top of their lungs, "My name is _____ and I love _____ !" Example: "My name is Aiden and I love trains!" Hold those high notes, opera-style!

- *Random Daily Dozen!* Stand up and do a dozen exercises. Feel free to mix them up if your kids have trouble sustaining twelve in a row, such as four jumping jacks, four squats, and four push-ups. (There's a mini math lesson there: 12 divided by 3, or 4 x 3, or 4 + 4 + 4, whatever math facts your child is working on.) You or your kids can make up your own exercise and show the family how to do a dozen.

- *Caucus Race!* Everybody gets up, runs around the table three times, and sits back down in the same place.

- *SUB Watch!* Preselect a short online video of something they might be interested in, such as how something is made in a factory, a domino run, or a marble race. Each child gets to choose one of 3 SUB ways to watch it: Standing, Upside down, or Bouncing.

- *If you're Aspie and you know it, flap your hands!* "Everybody flap! Bounce and flap! Flap up high! Flap to the side! Flap down low! Flap like so!" Each person can take their turn directing the rest of the family to join in a favorite stim. Change up the song to fit the feeling and the stim: "If you're _____ and you know it, _____."

- *Random LEGO® Challenge!* Give each child a plastic bag with a dozen plain LEGO® bricks (no fancy pieces) and tell them to put them together as quickly as they can. Bonus cheer for whoever finishes first and for each child who comes up with a name or purpose for their random creation. Good for fine motor practice and creative thinking!

- *Mystery Treasure Hunt!* Unbeknownst to them, make a video of a parent in disguise, giving them a mysterious treasure hunt assignment. Give a hint about where to find the first clue in the video and let each clue lead to another one, which you, of course, have hidden while they were sleeping. When you think they need a break, play the video and let them follow the clues to find a special snack or treat. Bonus points for you if you use their spelling words in the clues or require math to figure out the next location.

- *Nature Show!* If your pets wander into your home classroom, have the kids narrate their actions as if they're making a nature documentary. No pets? No problem! They can narrate what the neighborhood squirrel or songbird is up to. Live animals in short supply? Turn on a nature show and mute the sound so they can describe what they see. Let them narrate what you're doing as you make their lunch, or take turns being the animal and the narrator. Remember to use your poshest British accent!

I'm sure you can think of many more fun activities to put in your FART hat. Ask your older kids or other family members to come up with ideas, too. Remember your child's special sensitivities and passions when you plan these. If you have a kid who hates loud noises, then do not spring Random Dance music on them at full volume without warning. After you declare a Random Dance Party, let the sound-sensitive child be the one to turn on the music and set the volume before everyone rocks out. If you have kids with particular passions, consider using that passion as a theme for some of your random activities. If you have a LEGO® enthusiast, be sure to use the Random LEGO® Challenge. If they love trains or dinosaurs or cats, use the SUB Watch with a video featuring their favorite things. You can tailor your Frequent, Unscheduled, New activities to fit what is fun for your family. Enjoy!

> **SIOBHAN'S STRATEGIES:** Field Trips are a fun change to the daily grind at traditional school, so why not have them for homeschool? If your local zoo, aquarium, or museum has a free or reduced price day that you could never take advantage of because your kids were in school, now's your chance! If you schedule the kids' academic work accordingly, you can take a whole day off to unwind and reset.

PART IV

KIDS:

Keep Individualizing for Different Styles

"Everybody is different. Everybody deserves to be given an individual plan that's best suited for them."
— *Johnny Almaraz, baseball talent evaluator*

CHAPTER 13: DISTRACTIBLE DORY

"1, 2, 3, 4, 5 ... I love sand!"

— Dory from *Finding Dory*, Pixar

Do you have a Dory in your household? Dory has a "remembery" problem and is easily distracted by everything around her. If this sounds like one of your kids, help your little Dory FOCUS: Fidget appropriately, Observe others, Center, Underline what's important, and Stay on course. Here's how:

> *Fidget* appropriately. Having a small fidget object to hold can be helpful when trying to focus on a speaker. You don't have to go out and buy a specialty fidget if you don't want to. A fidget can be just about anything: a paper clip, a small pebble, an eraser, a bean bag, or a tiny plastic animal. However, if the fidget becomes a toy, it should be put away with the other toys until play time. How do you know the difference? Check out the object in the chart on the next page. Is it a fidget or is it a toy? Toys go away until later. No one's in trouble; it's just that toys don't belong in the classroom, even if your classroom is the kitchen table. Look for something else that could be a true fidget, and try again. Remember, the purpose of the fidget is to keep their hands busy so their minds can focus on learning. And, if you have more than one child you're homeschooling, you don't want your Dory to distract your other learners with an over-active fidget toy.

> *Observe* what others are doing. Sometimes our Dory can be blissfully unaware of what's going on around her, which is a good way to get lost, or at least lost in thought. Have her look around and ask what everyone else is doing. Working? Then ask what she is doing. Looking out the window at the birds? Parents always say, "If everybody

IT'S A FIDGET IF:	IT'S A TOY IF:
Attention is on the task.	Attention is on the object.
Object is silent.	Object squeaks or makes any audible sound.
Others in the room don't notice the object.	Everyone's attention is drawn to the object.
Object stays in their hands.	Object is thrown, bounced, or rolled.
Eyes are on the teacher-parent.	Eyes are on the object.

else jumped off a cliff, would you do it?" and if the other kids are jumping off a cliff, we don't want to encourage Dory to do the same. However, most of the time it's wise to observe and imitate others. If the other kids are working, setting the table for dinner, or getting on their jackets for a trip to the park, then that's a clue that Dory should do the same.

➤ *Center.* Use mindfulness techniques for centering to screen out distractions. These include closing the eyes, relaxing the shoulders and any other tense body parts, breathing in through the nose slowly for a count of four and out through the mouth for another four count. After several relaxing breaths, Dory will be better able to focus on what's important.

➤ *Underline* what's important. If she's looking for the main idea sentence in a paragraph, she might want to actually underline it. However, for most activities, it will be better to imagine it. What's important to think about and do right now? Once she knows what that is, from observing others to checking her schedule, she can say to herself, "I need to finish this paper," and imagine herself drawing a line under the words for emphasis. She can even close her eyes and draw a line in the air with her finger if it helps her focus.

➤ *Stay* on course. Now that she knows what to focus on, she needs to stay on course. This can be done with reminder sticky notes on her desk that say "Focus" or "What's important?" If she has a favorite superhero or character, consider making a card with a picture of them reminding her, such as "Spider-Man says, 'Stick with it!'" or "Thomas says, 'Stay on the right track!'" And, of course, "Dory says, 'Just keep swimming!'"

Whatever tips or tricks work best for your distractible Dory, use them to help her keep swimming, swimming, swimming. She can FOCUS by using Fidgets, Observing others to see what they're doing, Centering herself to screen out distractions, Underlining what's important, and Staying on course until the job is done.

> **SIOBHAN'S STRATEGIES:** Admit it: you still remember "P. Sherman 42 Wallaby Way, Sydney." It's not a bad thing—we all do. Repetition works. It's how you memorize a phone number, learned the alphabet, and get song lyrics stuck in your head. If you're trying to teach your Dory their new homeschool schedule, try repetition. You can make it a chant or song if you want. "Starting at 9, it's reading time!" Or, "Lunch, Zoom, Math, Art. Later there might be a FART!" Keep repeating it. You don't have to make it rhyme, but why wouldn't you?

CHAPTER 14: HYPER-FOCUSED HERMIONE

"Actually I'm highly logical, which allows me to look past extraneous detail and perceive clearly that which others overlook."
— Hermione Granger in *Harry Potter and the Deathly Hallows*
by J. K. Rowling

Do you have a high-strung, hyper-focused Hermione in your household? She's the one who has memorized all the schedules and rules and feels responsible for letting everyone know when they step a toe over the line.

Flexibility is not her strong suit, and she has trouble coping with change. Help your Hermione deal with unexpected transitions by making a "Surprise!" icon or sticky note for the schedule. Then, when she points out that stopping math to watch the geese migrating overhead is not on the schedule, you can put it on.

Hermione is highly rule-governed. She can't seem to let go of the smallest infraction. If you have a schedule and you stray from it by even five minutes, she is the one to remind you that 9:00 does not mean 9:05! Just as her classmates may have cringed when she reminded the teacher to give homework, so in homeschooling her siblings may cringe when she points out that it's bedtime and the movie needs to be turned off.

Those are the two biggest challenges Hermione faces: lack of flexibility and being overly rule-governed. To deal with them she needs to RELAX and CHILL.

By RELAX, we mean that when faced with unexpected change, she can Reset, Embrace change, Lighten up, Adjust to the new plan, and eXpand her horizon to increase flexibility.

> ➤ **Reset.** Sometimes the unexpected happens and ruins your carefully planned schedule. While most people can easily adjust and move on,

Hermione can't help but get stuck and may start spiraling. It's time to hit the Reset button. Try coaching your Hermione to develop calming mantras. Instead of saying "This is terrible!" try saying "This is different, and it's okay," or "This is unexpected, but it's not bad."

➤ *Embrace change.* Things will always change in life, so why not embrace it? Rather than let something new spoil the whole day, go all in with accepting it. You don't have a magical time-turner, so there's no use wishing you could go back. Maybe this change is the best thing that could happen!

➤ *Lighten up.* Use mindfulness and relaxation techniques to lighten up when under the stress of unexpected change. Remember to breathe, in through the nose for a count of four, out through the mouth for a count of four. Relax your tense muscles. Shake out your arms or hands, if that helps. Engage in your most calming stims. Pet your cat. Remember, the way to defeat the Devil's Snare is to be calm, but light also works! Maybe spend some time in the sun for a bit of light reading.

➤ *Adjust* to the inevitable. If a situation can't be changed, then we change to meet it. No, I'm not talking about Polyjuice Potion. Maybe the Wi-Fi went out and there's no way anyone can turn in their assignments before they're due. Breathe. Adjust. Go for a walk. When the Wi-Fi is back, you can send the work along with an email to the teachers explaining the lateness. The best you can do is literally the best you can do.

➤ *EXpand.* Every change brings an opportunity to expand what they're comfortable with. Each time your kid copes with something new and unexpected, they enlarge their repertoire of what they can handle. If book 1 Hermione had to face the things book 7 Hermione faced, she would have failed. The lessons she learned along the way expanded her abilities and experiences, just like with real kids. The world keeps expanding and growing, and your children are learning and growing right along with it. Congratulate them! Celebrate their expanded abilities! Maybe you can throw a House Cup celebration at the end of the semester to reward your kids for all they've accomplished.

CHILL can help Hermione cool her over-adherence to rules by teaching her to Check herself, Hear both sides, Ignore the impulse to control, Learn to listen, and Leave the litigation to the lawyers.

> ➤ *Check* yourself before you wreck yourself. Is Hermione trying to make other people obey all the house rules to the letter? Make it clear: Parents make the rules, and they are the ones to enforce them. Parents can also decide when leniency is appropriate. Has Hermione created her own rules that she thinks everyone should adhere to? There is no Prefect and no Head Girl or Head Boy in homeschool. She's not the boss of other people, so she doesn't get to make rules for everyone, even if it feels right to her.

> ➤ *Hear* both sides. Do the parents have reasons why they are loosening up on the rules today? Hermione needs to hear them out. They are the adults in the household, and they are in charge. Parents look at the big picture and make decisions for the family to keep everyone safe and happy. Kids can explain their position, but they also need to listen. Once both sides have been heard, parents have the last word.

> ➤ *Ignore the impulse* to control. This is not easy for Hermione. The desire to control the environment, which includes the other people in the household, is a powerful need. Are there areas where she can be given control? Find opportunities for her to be in charge of something. Perhaps she can choose what order she does her academic work in or what kind of P.E. activities she does. Provide her with many opportunities for control while reminding her to ignore the impulse to control what is not hers. Repeating an affirmation to herself such as "That is not my business, and that's okay" can help.

➤ *Learn to listen* to others. Hermione may believe she has all the answers and makes the smartest choices for everyone, but listening is an important skill to develop and encourage. Practice back-and-forth conversations where she must take turns and listen to her conversational partner. Then, she should make an on-topic comment or ask a pertinent question about what her partner said before she says her piece. Listen to understand, not just to respond.

➤ *Leave the litigation to the lawyers!* Perhaps one day Hermione will graduate from law school, and her innate talent for argument will pay off. Until that day, everyone in the household will be happier if she can learn to let go of the need to be right. She does not need to lecture her family as if she were an attorney presenting a summation to the jury. Social stories or narratives about minding one's own business can be helpful.

Strategies such as these can help your high-strung Hermione to RELAX and cope with change, and to be CHILL when the world does not accept her authority. These are uncertain times, and when we don't know what to expect, we can all feel a bit like Hermione, trying to control whatever we can. Moderation and acceptance help the family cope together.

> **SIOBHAN'S STRATEGIES:** Hermione tends to turn into a mini-mom or teacher's assistant if not otherwise occupied. If your Hermione is getting a little too helpful with her siblings' schoolwork, assign them workspaces in different parts of the house so she can't monitor what the others are doing. If you don't have room to do this, try alternating their schedules so she's busy elsewhere during the other kids' class time. Chores, free reading, or arts and crafts— whatever keeps her from bossing around her siblings the way she micromanages Ron's pronunciation of Levi-OH-sa.

CHAPTER 15: CREATIVE CALVIN

"It's only work if somebody makes you do it."

— Calvin to Hobbes, Bill Watterson

Albert Einstein said, "I have no special talent. I am only passionately curious." You may recognize your own highly creative Calvin in this sentiment. You know the many extraordinary places his curiosity carries him. If you give him a task and try to make him do it, he drags his feet and resists with all his might. However, if he gets an idea that sparks his curiosity, he has endless, unchained creative energy.

That math paper on his desk may remind him of origami, and while he's folding it into a paper crane, he remembers that cranes are migratory. What if they are flying overhead right now? So he's out the door, gazing up at the sky, where a cloud looks like an elephant. Where did he put that elephant book he'd been reading? Back in the house, he pulls all the books off the shelf looking for it but finds a book about insects instead. Termites, he reads, eat wood. Are there termites in the house right now? Could they be eating the wooden shelves in the pantry? Investigation is needed! First, Calvin must remove all the food from the shelves and climb way back in to where the termites are probably lurking, behind the baking soda and vinegar. That reminds Calvin of the volcano he made for science last year. What else could he do with vinegar and baking soda? He's just about to investigate when you come in and ask him if he's done with that math page yet ... Uh, no, he's not.

How can you hope to corral your creative Calvin and keep him moving forward rather than sideways and all over the place? Through ART: Accept, Reinforce, Transform.

> *Accept* alternative ways to meet the same goal. Accelerate his learning if he's ready for and interested in going beyond his grade level in a particular favorite subject. Allow creative responses. Would he rather write a play than a paragraph, then perform it with puppets? Go for it! Would he prefer to do fractions with LEGOS®, or money management via an internet pretend shopping spree? Let him! (Just keep your bank password protected. Safety first!) While we're talking about acceptance, let's remember to accept your child's imaginary friends. Lots of kids have them, like Calvin had Hobbes. Don't be concerned if your child talks to their toys or pets, and don't worry that they are too old for such things. They may be practicing their conversational skills on a friend who won't make fun of them or getting their social needs met without leaving home. So, relax. Once you accept and accommodate his unique learning style, your Calvin will amaze and astonish you with his creativity!

> *Reinforce* his explorations as he dives headfirst into new subjects. Share his excitement in learning new things on many different topics. He has a wonderful mind, and given free rein (within reason), his artistic ideas will delight you. Praise him for the awesome way his brain works and the creative directions it takes him!

> *Transform* ordinary assignments into productions. Let him form a university and teach a new concept to his younger siblings, pets, or action figures. He will learn it better than if he simply read the textbook and answered the questions at the end of the chapter. If he makes a museum or writes a poem or creates a mural about curriculum topics rather than just reading about them, he will retain the concepts far better and longer. And if you can document his work through pictures or videos, he will have a permanent reminder he can look back on with pride.

SIOBHAN'S STRATEGIES: Calvin loves using his creativity to transform a simple cardboard box into just about anything. Remember when he made a Time Machine? Good, because you're going to help your Calvin make one. Decorate a usable cardboard box—it doesn't have to be big enough to fit him, but it has to be able to hold several things without the bottom falling out. Take a picture of his genius invention and put it on his visual schedule after academic time is through. Now, whenever you catch Calvin off-task, whatever he's playing with goes in the Time Machine, to be accessed at another time. Is that a harmonica you hear playing upstairs? Sounds like it belongs in the Time Machine! Is he rummaging through the recycling looking for robot parts? Time Machine! Walk into the kitchen and find him wearing a colander on his head and filling the turkey baster? Dude, Time Machine! When school is over and the schedule commands, he gets to take all those creative things out of the box. This way, you're not saying "No" to his ideas; you're saying everything has a time, just not right now. If he's forgotten what he wanted to do with his baseball bat, some oranges, and a snorkel, that's fine. Give him a countdown to either come up with a new idea or put it all away. Keep a running list of things which are incompatible with time travel technology (living beings, food that would spoil, car keys, fire extinguishers) that must be put back right away instead of waiting in the Time Machine.

With just enough supervision for safety's sake, you can use ART to help your creative Calvin turn ordinary schoolwork into amazing, unforgettable experiences. Remember to Accept alternate ways of learning, Reinforce his channeled creativity, and Transform his learning experiences. He could never have accomplished all this in a traditional classroom setting. Because you are homeschooling, the sky is no longer the limit. Your child's imagination is the only limit, and it is boundless. Kudos to you for making this possible. Enjoy going along for the ride!

PART V

END:
Educate, Navigate, Demonstrate

CHAPTER 16: THE END OF THE BOOK.

You Can Take It from Here.

"The reward of a thing well done is having done it."
— Ralph Waldo Emerson

We reach the end of this book, but it's really the beginning of your homeschooling adventure. As a reminder of what we've been learning here, when you think of the END, think Educate, Navigate, Demonstrate.

EDUCATE

➤ *Teachable moments* are all around you; be ready for side trips.

➤ *Individualize* based on each child's strengths, passions, and needs.

➤ *Balance* the need for structure with the need for flexibility.

NAVIGATE

➤ *Plan B.* Be prepared to change your lesson plan when you run into roadblocks.

➤ *Side Trips.* Be ready to dive deeper into a subject that sparks their interest rather than sticking to the main road.

➤ *Patience* is paramount. Everybody is under stress, and if they need a moment or more than a moment, be generous.

DEMONSTRATE

➤ *Model the response you want to see.* If you want your children to respond to disappointment with maturity and self-control, model it for them. They will learn more from your actions than from your words.

➤ *Be the kind of person you want to raise.* Jim Henson said, "(Kids) don't remember what you tried to teach them. They remember what you are." Live your life as a demonstration of your morals and values. They're watching and learning.

Before we go, let's talk about stress one more time. We've all got it, and uncertain times increase and magnify it. Remember to take care of yourselves and each other. Extra patience and kindness go a long way.

In Uppsala, Sweden, there's a curious little ritual that college kids use to relieve stress during final exams known as the Flogsta Scream. Every night during finals week, students open their dorm room windows at 10 PM and scream into the night. Now, I must inform you that neither the authors of this book nor Future Horizons, Inc. publishers condone screaming out of your window at 10 PM on a school night, but there are other ways to reduce stress.

Every day in the age of Corona is stressful. Sometimes you feel like you've just got to scream. As Fuji-Q Highland Amusement Park told their roller coaster riders, "Please scream inside your heart." If that doesn't do it for you, try this SCREAM: Soothing sensory stimulation, Creativity, Read, Exercise, Ask for help, Meditate. Doing at least one of these each day can help prevent kid meltdowns and parent breakdowns.

SCREAM

➤ *Soothing sensory stimulation.* Relax and stimulate your senses. *Sight*: Hang twinkling lights and pictures of their passions. Watch videos of cute animals, marble races, soap cutting, domino runs, power washing, or the rain forest. *Sound*: Music is the obvious choice, but don't discount rain sticks, videos of babies laughing, waterfalls, or ASMR: autonomous sensory meridian response. *Touch*: Put on your cozy socks, relax under a soft weighted blanket, and stroke your pets. *Taste*: Obviously we're going to eat, but some things are extra special treats. If someone has a particularly bad day, maybe they should choose what's for dessert or pick a favorite restaurant for a takeout dinner. *Smell*: Aromatherapy is a staple of spas for a reason. Let your kids take turns picking a scented candle to burn (safely, under supervision), or vote for their favorite scent if you buy air fresheners. In our house, the most popular aromatherapy devices are a plug-in scented wax melter (no smoke or open flame) and our Instant Pot. We love the aroma of a savory soup or stew simmering away! Baking cookies, a vase of flowers, or fresh-cut fruit can all be delightful sources of soothing smells. SAFETY ALERT: Essential oil diffusers can cause dangerous reactions in pets. Since there is no definitive database of which essential oils cause which symptoms in which animals, it's safer to avoid using them in rooms where pets are allowed. If you want to use essential oils and you have pets, stick to rollerball applications or sniffing scented items rather than air dispersal methods.

➤ *Creativity.* Creativity feeds the soul, for adults as well as kids. Hobbies, crafts, and art projects can soothe everyone, and you can create something that the family can enjoy for years. Performing music, poetry, or drama can build your child's confidence. Even personal creative endeavors that they don't want to share with the family can provide emotional benefits.

➤ *Read.* We're writers, so we might be biased, but our house has always been full of books, and it was natural to read every day. If your child needs to go explore the world for a while, but the world is still shut down, books are the answer. Fiction can take us to worlds that don't really exist, and travel books can show us the world we can't reach. Even if it's a book they've read a million times, let them read. It feels like a safe place when the world is scary. During these times of extensive trauma, your kids might be reaching for books you thought they outgrew years ago. Don't worry; they'll go back to reading at their own level later. Sometimes they need something that feels easy and comfortable, not a challenge.

➤ **Exercise.** Moving your body releases endorphins and can help unblock your brain. Our bodies are built to move, and we have the benefit of not being in a classroom or office, where people might judge us for taking a jump rope break. Here's the thing about stress: our brains don't know the difference between a midterm exam, a global pandemic, and a bear that wants to eat you. It assumes a physical response is necessary and fills you with stress hormones to power you through it. Your body doesn't realize that staying inside and washing your hands are the appropriate responses. Try some air boxing or go for a run, and see how much better you feel.

➤ **Ask for help.** This is a hard one. We all assume that we are self-sufficient, and our culture supports this idea. In reality, we are a social species, and we are meant to ask for help when we need it. Encourage your kids to ask for help when they need it by modeling the behavior yourself. Ask your family to make dinner some night if you need a break, even if that means you all have breakfast for dinner. Thank them for helping you. Ask your BFF to help you run an errand, and thank them for their help where your kids can overhear you. Ask the grandparents to help with a safe and physically distanced play date so you can be alone for an important Zoom meeting. And when your kids ask for help, reward the behavior by helping without judging.

➤ **Meditate.** A daily meditation practice can benefit the whole family. Your kids may have been practicing some form of meditation or quiet time in school already. The internet has many free resources for parents, such as guided imagery meditation videos aimed at children, printable labyrinth pages for kids to trace, and videos for moving meditations like yoga or tai chi. You can also coach your kids in simple, stress-relieving meditations that don't require any space or supplies. One simple breathing technique is to imagine smelling a flower while inhaling, then exhaling as if you're blowing out a candle. A common grounding technique is to use your five senses to identify 5 things you can see, either in the room or out the window; 4 things you can feel, like your clothes, the wind, or the floor; 3 things you can hear, like a barking dog or the air conditioner; 2 things you can smell, like your shampoo or tonight's dinner; and 1 thing you can taste, like toothpaste. If their answers include things you can't sense in the same environment, that's fine: most neurotypicals can't hear electricity, but most autists can. If they answer that the thing they can taste is their mouth, that's fine, too.

SIOBHAN'S STRATEGIES: If you've tried all of these and someone in the house still needs to scream, try this: warn the family (headphones and earplugs might come in handy), turn on some loud music (punk, emo, rap, and metal are all good for this), grab a pillow, and scream into it. Everyone is allowed to scream during the scream song. You can scream into your pillow in your room, in the closet, the basement, the garage, as long as you are close enough to hear the music. When the song is over, so is the screaming. Scream responsibly! If someone can't stop themselves when the song ends, then the pillow scream song technique might not be right for your family.

You can pick one of these activities to practice every day, or mix it up. The important thing is to regularly provide outlets for stress, so it doesn't build up and explode. If you have a favorite hobby or self-care practice you want to teach your family, do it. Ask everyone else if there's something they like to do to blow off steam that they can share. Their strategy might be effective for someone else. It's good to share what works. After all, we're all in this together.

Plato said, "Do not train a child to learn by force or harshness, but direct them to it by what amuses their minds, so that you may be better able to discover with accuracy the peculiar bent of the genius of each." Your little geniuses may not learn exactly like every other kid, but no one does. By giving them the gift of homeschooling, whether by choice or because of COVID-19, you give them a unique opportunity. Learning at home, they can pursue what amuses their minds and follow the leading of their imagination, at least for a portion of their school day. Make this year at home one that they will remember fondly for years to come.

HELPFUL BOOKS

Anderson, Lynette. (2020). *You Are a Superhero! A Children's Picture Book About the Coronavirus*. New York, NY: Barnes and Noble Press.

Ball, James & Brown-Lofland, Kristie. (2020). *Autism After the Pandemic: A Step-by-Step Guide to Successfully Transition Back to School and Work*. Arlington, TX: Future Horizons, Inc.

Ball, James. (2019). *You Can't Make Me! Pro-active Strategies for Positive Behavior Change in Children*. Arlington, TX: Future Horizons, Inc.

Brite, Lori. (2019). *The Angry Octopus: A Relaxation Story*, second edition. Marietta, GA: Stress Free Kids.

Future Horizons' Authors. (2020). *Autism in Lockdown: Expert Tips and Insights on Coping with the COVID Pandemic*. Arlington, TX: Future Horizons, Inc.

Gray, Carol. (2020). *COVID-19: I Can Help!* https://carolgraysocialstories.com/wp-content/uploads/2020/03/COVID-19-I-Can-Help-1.pdf.

Gray, Carol. (2015). *The New Social Stories Book, Revised and Expanded*. Arlington, TX: Future Horizons, Inc.

Haseltine, William A. (2020). *A Family Guide to COVID: Questions & Answers for Parents, Grandparents and Children*. New York, NY: Access Health International.

Huebner, Dawn. (2017). *Outsmarting Worry: An Older Kid's Guide to Managing Anxiety.* London, UK: Jessica Kingsley Publishers.

Huebner, Dawn. (2005). *What to do When you Worry Too Much: A Kid's Guide to Overcoming Anxiety.* Washington, DC: American Psychological Association.

Lewis, Natlee. (2020). *The Stay-at-Home Order: A COVID-19 Children's Series #1.* Natlee Lewis.

Marsh, Wendela Whitcomb. (2018). *The ABCs of Autism in the Classroom: Setting the Stage for Success.* Arlington, TX: Future Horizons, Inc.

Melmed, Raun & Wheeler, Maria. (2015). *Autism and the Extended Family: A Guide for Those Outside the Immediate Family who Know and Love Someone with Autism.* Arlington, TX: Future Horizons, Inc.

Melmed, Raun & Marsh, Wendela Whitcomb. (2020). *Autism Parent Handbook: Begin with the End Goal in Mind* (*TBD) Arlington, TX: Future Horizons, Inc.

Melmed, Raun & associates. (2016-2020). *Monster Diary Mindfulness Book Series.* Sanger, CA: Familias.

Notbohm, Ellen. (2019). *Ten Things Every Child with Autism Wishes You Knew,* 3rd edition. Arlington, TX: Future Horizons, Inc.

Pearl, Emma. (2020). C-19: *A Coronavirus Book for Kids, Parents & Grandparents.* San Francisco, CA: Blurb.

Phelan, Thomas W. *1-2-3 Magic: The Coronavirus Manual for Parents.* Naperville, IL: Sourcebooks, LLC.

Smith, Lolo. (2020). *Community Workers & COVID-19: A Children's Book About Coronavirus*. Edited by Marion D. Ingram and Rhonda Lee Thomas. Independently published.

Whittier, Kishon W. (2020). *Instead Say This ... For Parents During the Coronavirus Pandemic*. Olney, MD: White Pine Coaching, LLC.

Yacio, Jennifer Gilpin. (2020) *COVID-19 Isn't Fair!* Arlington, TX: Future Horizons, Inc.

Yacio, Jennifer Gilpin. (2015). *Temple Did It, and I Can, Too!* Seven Simple Life Rules. Arlington, TX: Future Horizons, Inc.

Youssef, Donia. (2020). *Monster in the Air: A Children's Storybook on the Coronavirus*. UK: Tiny Angel Press, Ltd.

AUTHOR BIOS

SIOBHAN MARSH

Siobhan is a disability advocate and Kay Snow Award-winning writer living in Salem, Oregon. Growing up with chronic illness that made on-campus education difficult, Siobhan completely restructured her homeschooling schedule and developed many strategies which she includes in this book, allowing her to fit in doctor's appointments, creative pursuits, and volunteer work while maintaining her GPA and graduating second in her class. She is also uniquely suited to discuss neurodiverse family life as the daughter and sister of autists.

WENDELA WHITCOMB MARSH

Wendela is an autism educator, speaker, consultant, and author of *The ABCs of Autism in the Classroom: Setting the Stage for Success* and *Independent Living with Autism: Your Roadmap to Success*. In addition, she contributed a chapter for *Autism in Lockdown: Expert Tips and Insights on Coping with the COVID-19 Pandemic*, and she co-authored with Dr. Raun Melmed *Autism Parent Handbook: Beginning with the End Goal in Mind*. Spouse and parent to awesome autists, she lives in Salem, Oregon with her three children and two cats. Learn more about her books at *www.wendelawhitcombmarsh.com* and about her consultation services at PIPS for Autism, LLC: Promoting Independence & Problem Solving, *www.pipsforautism.com*.

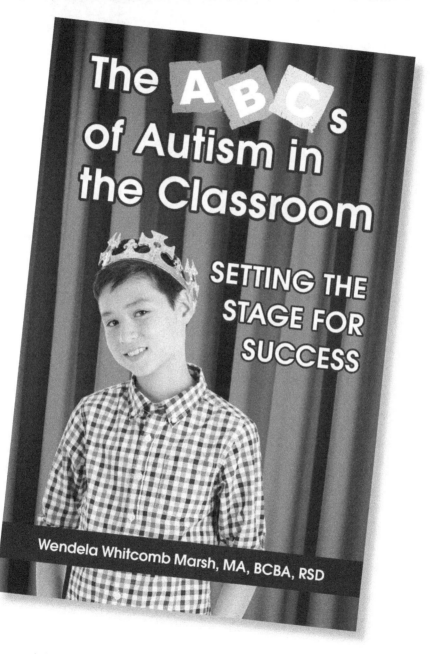

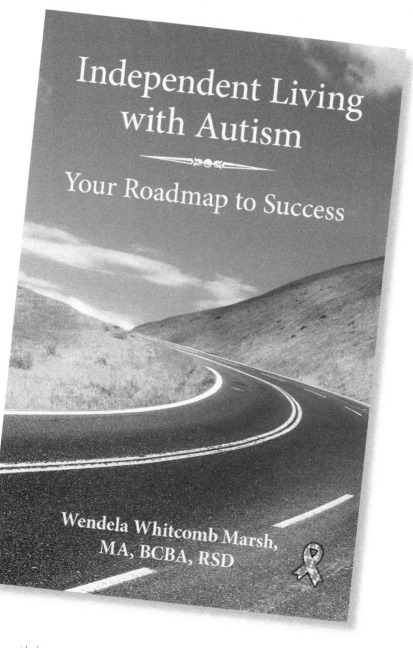

CPSIA information can be obtained
at www.ICGtesting.com
Printed in the USA
JSHW051755111020
8670JS00001B/1